Ways into Science

Keeping Healthy

Peter Riley

W
FRANKLIN WATTS
LONDON · SYDNEY

Franklin Watts
Published in Great Britain in 2016
by The Watts Publishing Group

Copyright images © Franklin Watts 2015
Copyright text © Peter Riley 2015
(Text has previously appeared in *Ways into Science: Keeping Healthy* (2003) but has been comprehensively re-written for this edition.)

All rights reserved.

Editor: Julia Bird
Designer: Basement 68

ISBN: 978 1 4451 3484 0
Dewey classification number: 610

Printed in China

Franklin Watts
An imprint of
Hachette Children's Group
Part of The Watts Publishing Group

Carmelite House
50 Victoria Embankment
London EC4Y 0DZ

An Hachette UK Company
www.hachette.co.uk
www.franklinwatts.co.uk

FSC
www.fsc.org
MIX
Paper from responsible sources
FSC® C104740

Photo acknowledgements: All photos Roy Moller for Franklin Watts except: Asife/Shutterstock: 7c. Hung Chung Chih/Shutterstock: 7c. Tim Dub/Photofusion: 5t, 18t. Tatiana Gladskikh/Shutterstock: 3,10t. g215/Shutterstock: 5c, 17b. Jorg Hackemann/Shutterstock: 17t. Matt Hayward/Shutterstock: 4, 27b. Carlos Horta/Shutterstock: 6. Sebastian Kaulitzki/Shutterstock: 14b. Lasse Kristensen/Shutterstock: 24cb. Nito/Shutterstock: 19c. Thomas Perkins/Dreamstime : 19t, 26bcl. Photollinc/Shutterstock: 10bc. Racorn/Dreamstime: 21b. Dimitriy Shironov/Dreamstime: 5ca, 19c. 3445128471/Shutterstock: 7t, 14t. Nico Trant/Shutterstock: 18b. Dani Vincek/Shutterstock: 10br. Volosina/Shutterstock: 10bl. WBB/Shutterstock: 8cr.
Every attempt has been made to clear copyright. Should there be any inadvertent omission, please apply to the Publishers for rectification.

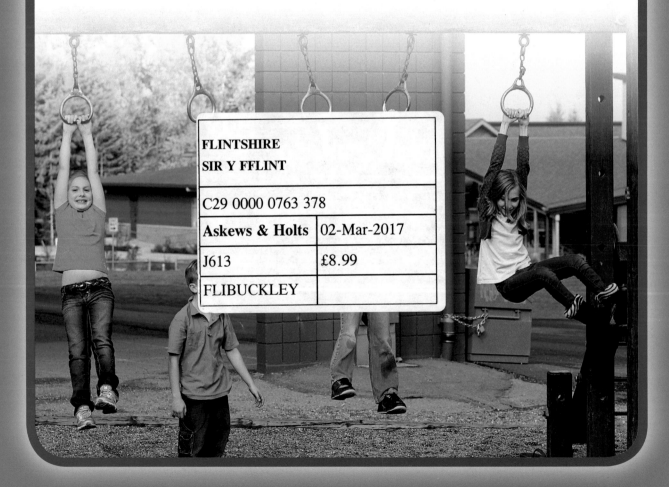

Contents

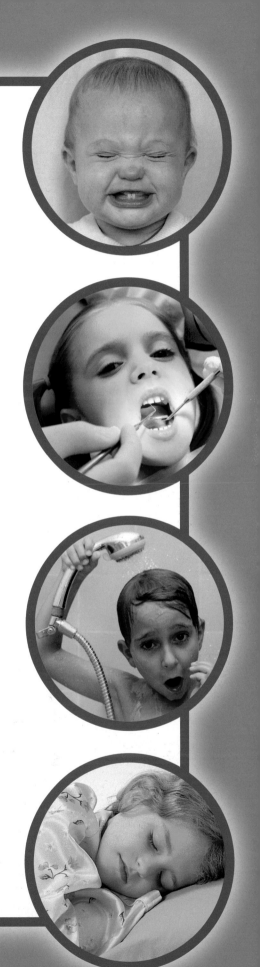

A healthy body

A healthy body helps you to stay well and happy.

Here are some ways to keep healthy.

Eating and drinking well.

Keeping clean.

Exercising.

Sleeping.

Why do you need food? Turn the page to find out.

7

Food

Our bodies work hard all the time. We need energy for everything we do. We get energy from food.

These foods contain large amounts of energy.

bread

potatoes

pasta

rice

oats

We need to eat different kinds of fruit and vegetables to keep well.

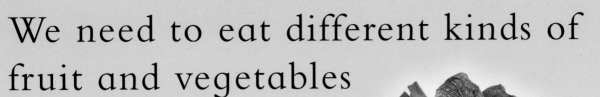

Which of these do you like to eat?

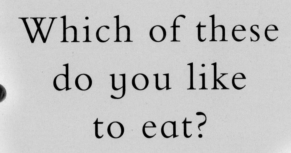

Which vegetables are on this kebab?

Why else do we need food? Turn the page to find out.

9

Food for growth

Everyone grows at their own rate.

These foods help people to grow.

eggs

cheese

lentils

meat

fish

beans

What do you eat to help you grow?

10

To stay healthy, you need foods for energy, keeping well and growth. You also need plenty to drink.

Sam and Hannah want to make a healthy meal.

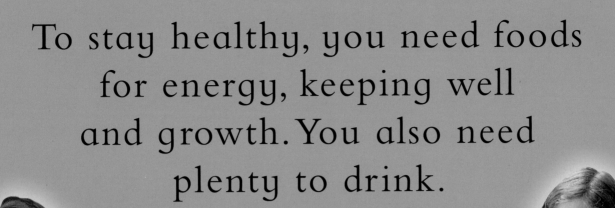

What should they choose? Turn the page to find out.

Healthy meals

Sam has chosen chicken, rice and vegetables. This meal has food for growth, energy and keeping well.

Here is another healthy meal.

salad

potato

cheese

Hannah has chosen a beefburger and some cheese. She has not chosen any foods for keeping well or for energy.

Here is another less healthy meal.

What should you always remember to do before you eat? Turn the page to find out.

Keeping clean

You should wash your hands before eating. You should also wash them after going to the toilet.

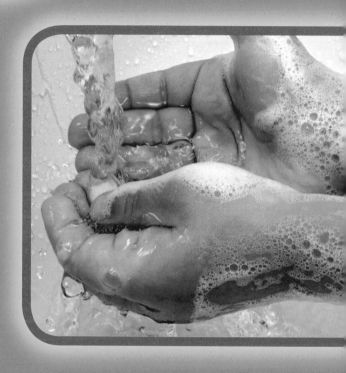

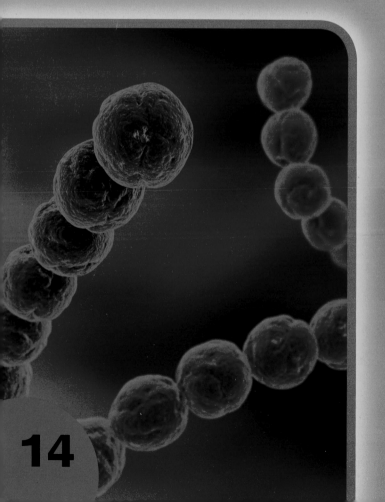

This is to wash away tiny living things called germs. You can only see germs through a powerful microscope.

Katie, Paul and Nicole have dirty hands. They each wash them for 15 seconds.

Katie uses cold water.

Paul uses cold water and soap.

Nicole uses warm water and soap.

Who will have the cleanest hands? Turn the page to find out.

15

Wash and dry

Nicole has the cleanest hands.

Hot water and soap are best for washing your hands. Remember to dry them afterwards!

The rest of your body needs a good wash too.

Your skin makes sweat to keep you cool. The sweat makes your skin dirty. Germs like to live in the dirt.

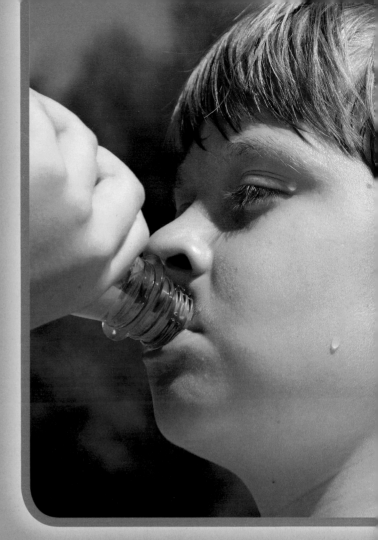

Wash your body every day to stop germs living on your skin.

What else should you wash every day? Turn the page to find out.

17

Teeth

You need to clean your teeth every day. This keeps them healthy so you can bite and chew food.

We have two sets of teeth. We get our first set at six months old – our milk teeth.

At about six years old, we begin to lose our milk teeth. Bigger, adult teeth take their place.

There are three ways to keep your teeth healthy.

1. Clean them in the morning and at night.

2. Try not to eat lots of sugary foods.

3. Visit the dentist twice a year.

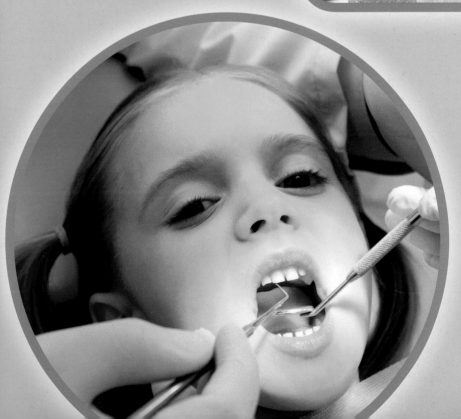

Exercise

Taking exercise also helps to keep your body healthy.

Exercise keeps your joints active.

Exercise also makes your muscles stronger.

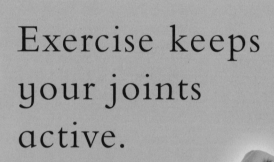

There are lots of ways to take exercise.

These children are going to school.

Hannah is walking to school.

Alex and James are going in the car.

?

Who is taking more exercise? Turn the page to find out.

Body parts

Hannah is exercising her arms and legs more by walking.

What parts of their body are Sarah, Tom and Sophie exercising?

Taking a rest

Sam and Nicole have been playing outside for an hour.

Why do you think they need to rest and have a drink and a snack?

What do we do when we rest at night? Turn the page to find out.

23

Sleep

We rest at night by sleeping. We need sleep to stay healthy.

When we sleep, our bodies rest. We have more energy when we wake up.

If we do not get enough sleep, we feel tired and grumpy.

If we get enough sleep, we feel fit and lively.

How long do you sleep? Make a table like this and fill it in.

Day	Lights out	Wake up	Hours of sleep
Monday	8.00pm	7.00am	11
Tuesday	?	?	?
Wednesday	?	?	?
Thursday	?	?	?
Friday	?	?	?
Saturday	?	?	?
Sunday	?	?	?

Healthy and happy

It is fun to have a healthy lifestyle.

Fill in the table to find out if you have a healthy lifestyle.

Lifestyle check	Always	Usually	Never
Do you eat healthy meals?	✗	✓	✗
Do you wash your hands before eating?	?	?	?
Do you wash your whole body every day?	?	?	?
Do you brush your teeth every day?	?	?	?
Do you exercise every day?	?	?	?
Do you go to bed late?	?	?	?

Do you have a healthy lifestyle?

What are these children doing to stay healthy?

Where do they get their energy from?

What must they do before they eat a meal?

Useful words

Adult teeth – the second set of teeth. There are thirty-two adult teeth.

Dentist – a person whose job it is to look after your teeth.

Disease – something that makes you feel unwell.

Energy – the power we get from food, which makes us able to keep warm and be active.

Exercise – movements of the body.

Germs – tiny living things that can spread disease and make you feel ill. Germs are too small to see.

Healthy – being fit and well.

Joint – a place in the body where two bones fit together.

Lentil – a kind of dry seed.

Lifestyle – the way a person lives.

Microscope – a tool that makes it possible for us to see tiny things.

Milk teeth – the first set of teeth. There are twenty milk teeth.

Muscle – a part of the body that can move and makes other parts move.

Sweat – a salty liquid that comes out of your skin when your body is hot.

Some answers

Here are some answers to the questions we have asked in this book. Don't worry if you had some different answers to ours: you may be right too. Talk through your answers with other people and see if you can explain why they are right.

Page 9 The vegetables on the kebab are onion, courgette, mushroom and pepper.

Page 22 Sarah is exercising her arms, Tom is exercising his arms and legs, but mainly his legs. Sophie is exercising her legs.

Page 23 Sam and Nicole need to replace the energy that they have used up while playing outside.

Page 26 A person who has a healthy lifestyle ticks all the boxes in the always column. A person with an unhealthy life style ticks all the boxes in the never column. Most people usually have a healthy lifestyle.

Page 27 These children are exercising their bodies to stay healthy. They get their energy from the food they eat. They must wash their hands before they eat a meal.

Index

About this book

Ways into Science is designed to encourage children to think about their everyday world in a scientific way and to make investigations to test their ideas. There are five lines of enquiry that scientists make in investigations. These are grouping and classifying, observing over time, making a fair test, searching for patterns and researching using secondary sources.

When children open this book they are already making one line of enquiry – researching about the body. As they read through the book they are invited to make other lines of enquiry and to develop skills in scientific investigation.

• On pages 8–10 they learn how to classify foods.

• On page 9 they must use observational skills to identify the vegetables on the kebab.

• On page 11 they use the information on this page and the previous three pages to make a prediction.

• On page 15 they examine information about a fair test and make a prediction.

• On page 21 they make a comparison and use it as the basis for a prediction.

• On page 25 they make a table, record the times of going to sleep and waking and present them in the table.

• On page 26 they should make a copy of the table and, observing their behaviour over time, fill it in.

• On page 27 they should draw a conclusion based on the data in the table on page 26 and the information in the book.